LISTEN TO YOUR ART

A guided journaling adventure

By YOU

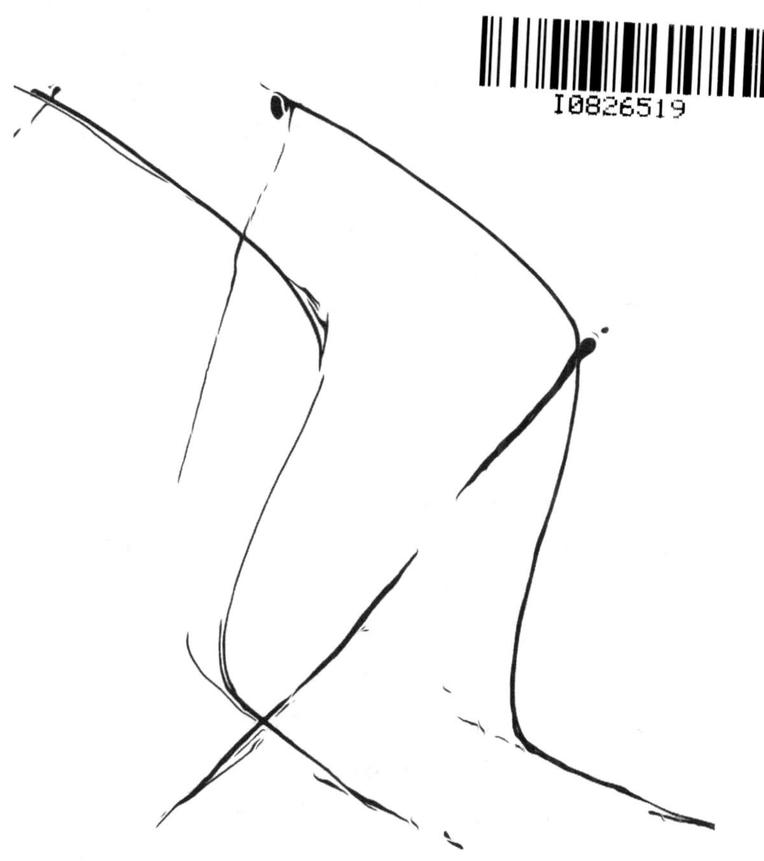

With love Jordan Raye

Welcome....

This guided journaling book was created for you to have a safe space for self expression, exploration and discovery. You can use this book as a daily practice and tool to get clarity, guidance, perspective and answers on situations, relationships or patterns in your life. There are no rules here. Below is a suggestion on how you can use this book for your benefit. If there's another way that works better for you then do that! Remember it's YOUR journey.

How does it work ....

Start by taking a few deep breaths. Close your eyes while holding this book, ask a question or just simply ask for guidance. When you feel ready, randomly open the book to any page. Look at the image on the page you have selected, rotating it and looking at it from different angles, see what images come up for you. Take your time. You might see a few different images but choose one that you keep coming back to. Once you choose an image ,color it in giving it life. You can add any thing you like. Use markers, pens, pencils, paint.

Do whatever feels right and try acting on your initial thoughts and intuition. Staying present in each step. Once you are happy with your creation answer the questions on the next page. When writing your answers, try to write whatever comes to mind, even if it doesn't make sense,the key here is not to overthink. Just write as much as you can staying in the flow.

What is free writing ....

It is a writing process that involves continuously writing without overthinking, editing or worrying about grammar. It's being fully present in the flow of writing and allowing whatever comes to mind go on the page. Free writing can be freeing and insightful, helping us to discover new ideas, thoughts, emotions and boost our self awareness.

Final words:

Have fun, dare to be silly, dare to be honest, invite in any feelings, thoughts and ideas that show up. This experience is only between you and and yourself.

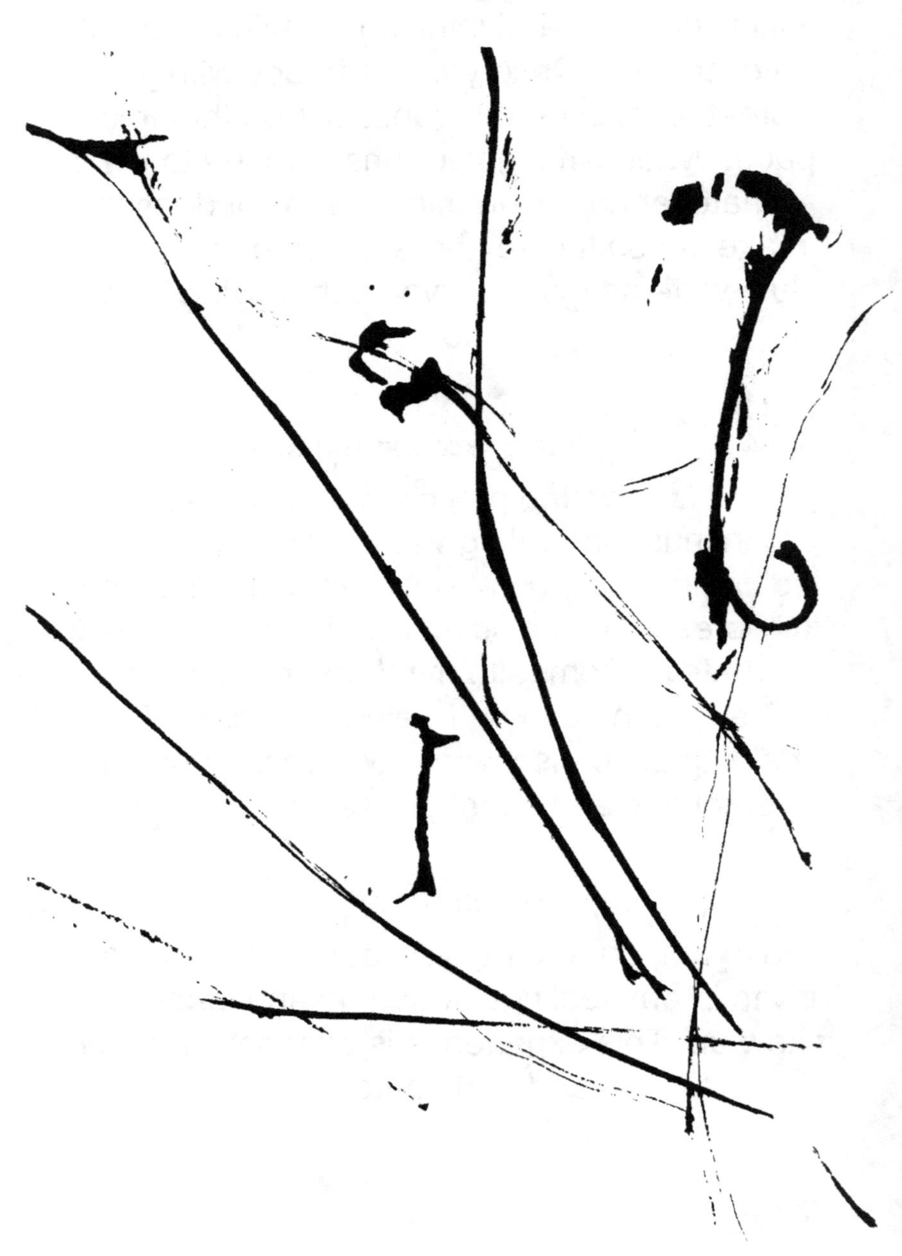

My name is ...

I am the messenger of ...

I am here to tell you ...

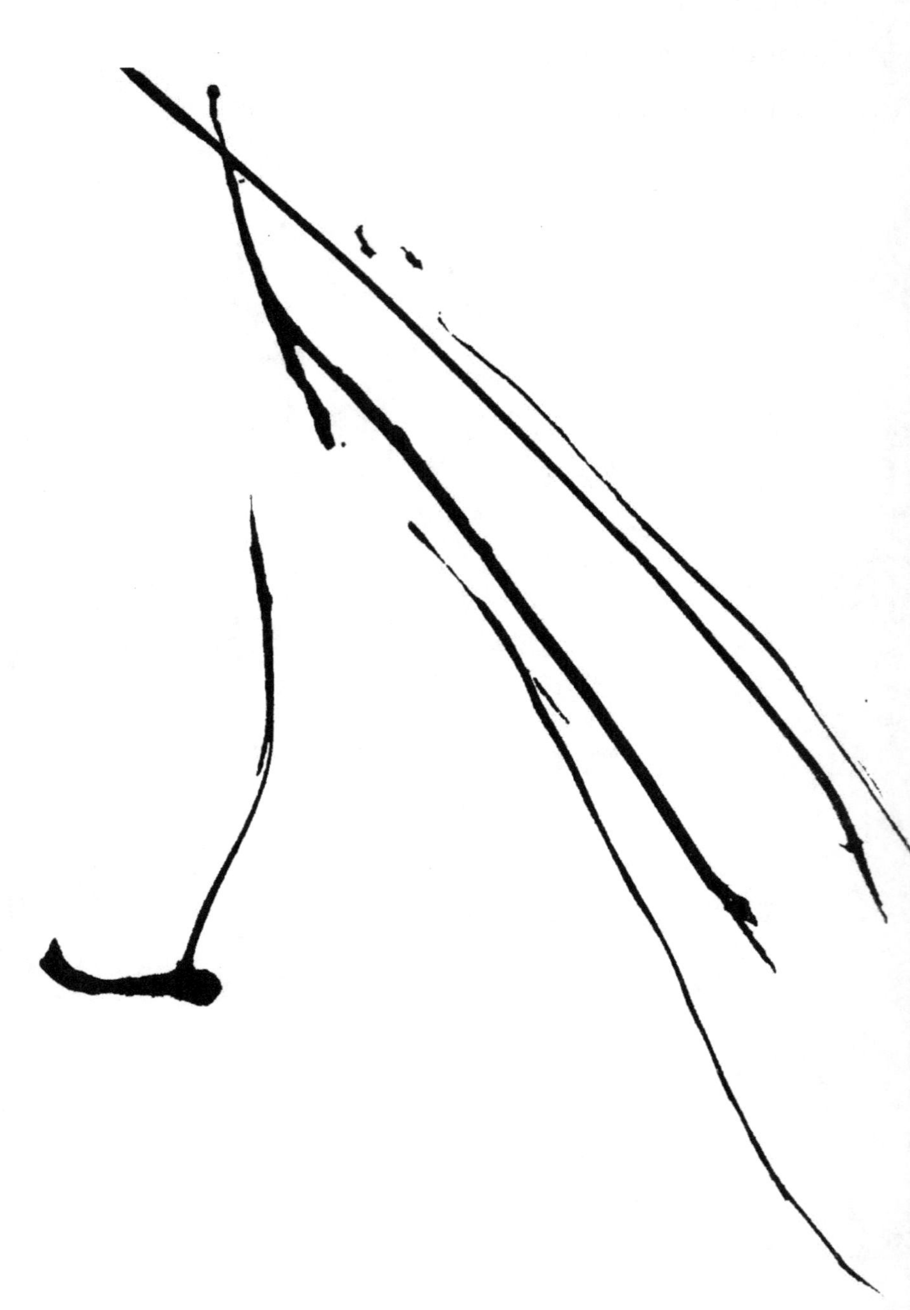

My name is ...

I am the messenger of ...

I am here to tell you ...

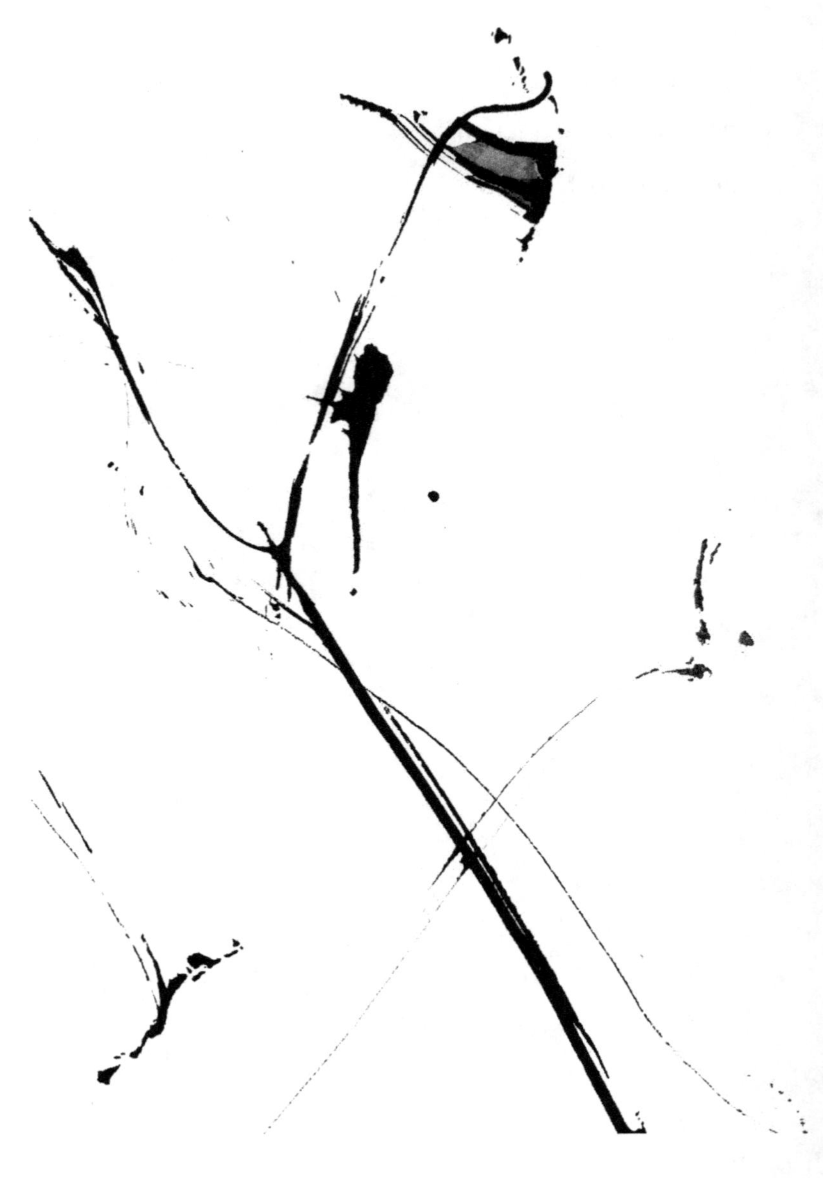

My name is ...

I am the messenger of ...

I am here to tell you ...

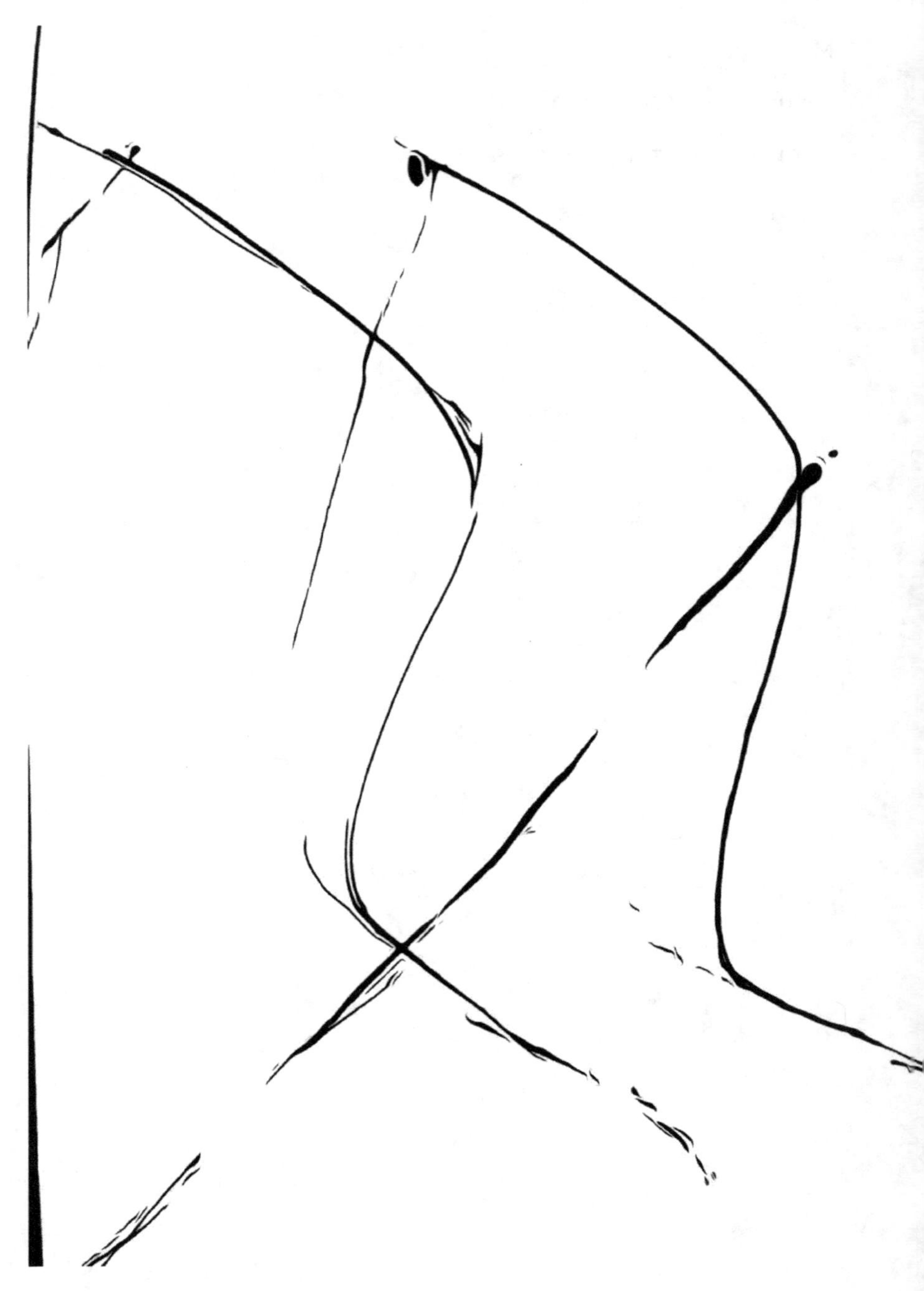

My name is ...

I am the messenger of ...

I am here to tell you ...

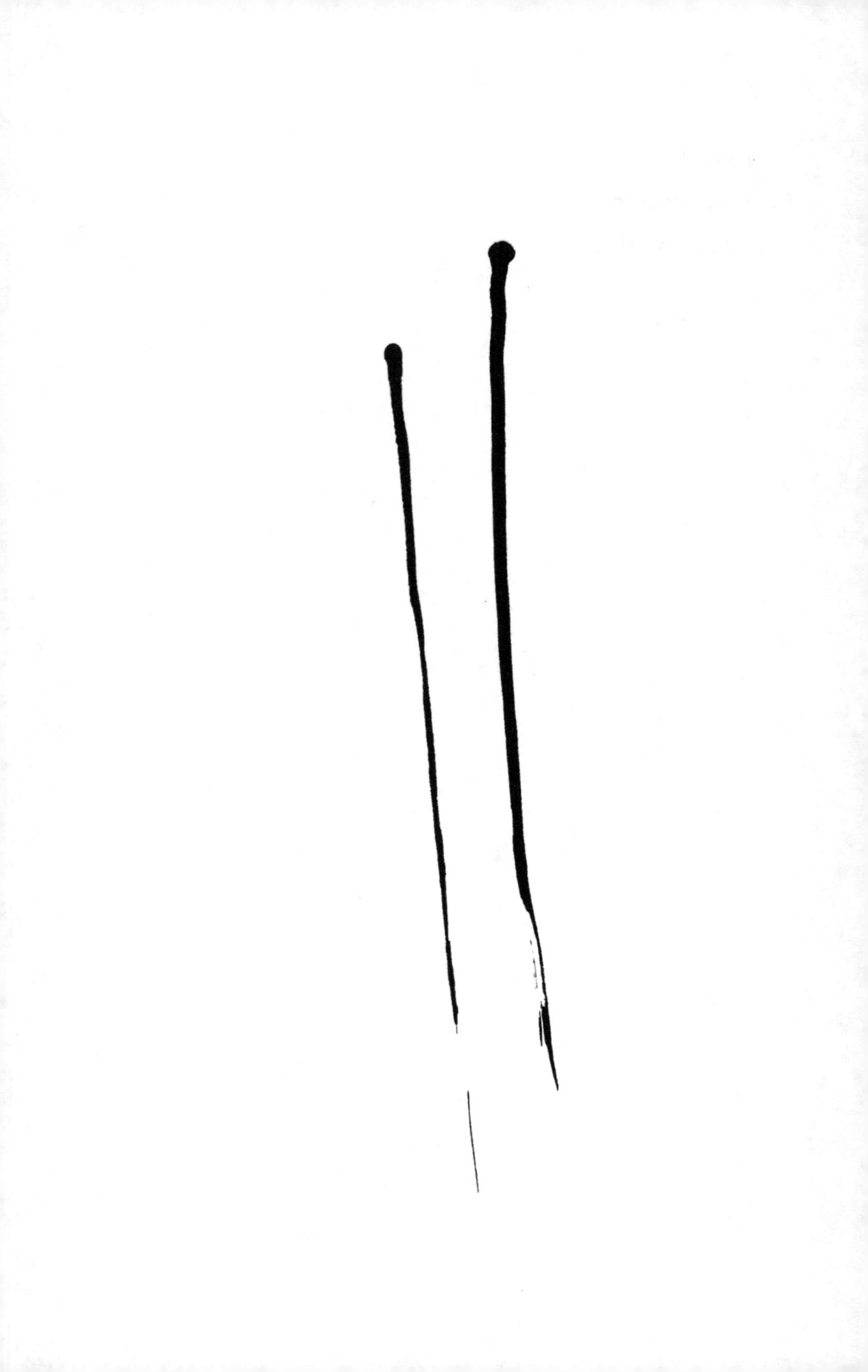

My name is ...

I am the messenger of ...

I am here to tell you ...

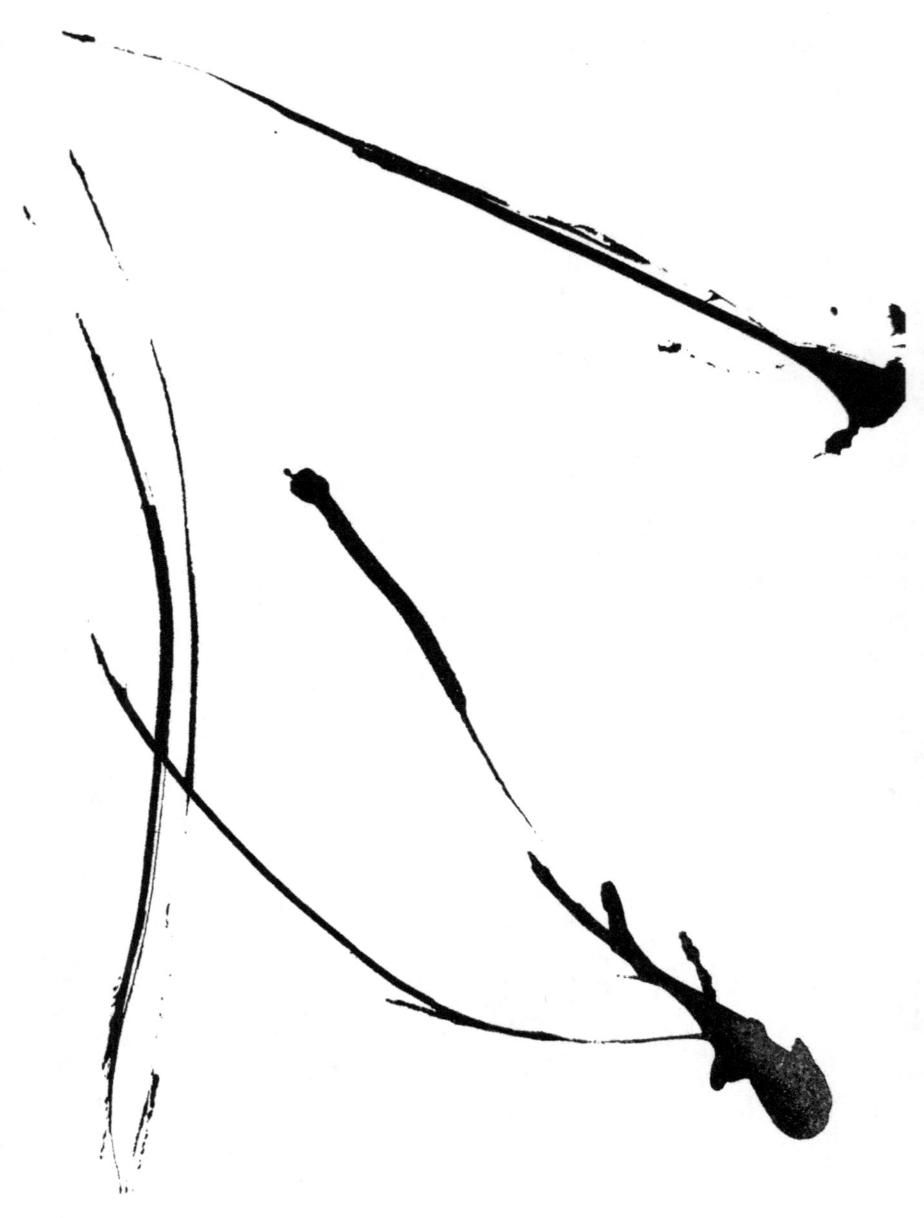

My name is ...

I am the messenger of ...

I am here to tell you ...

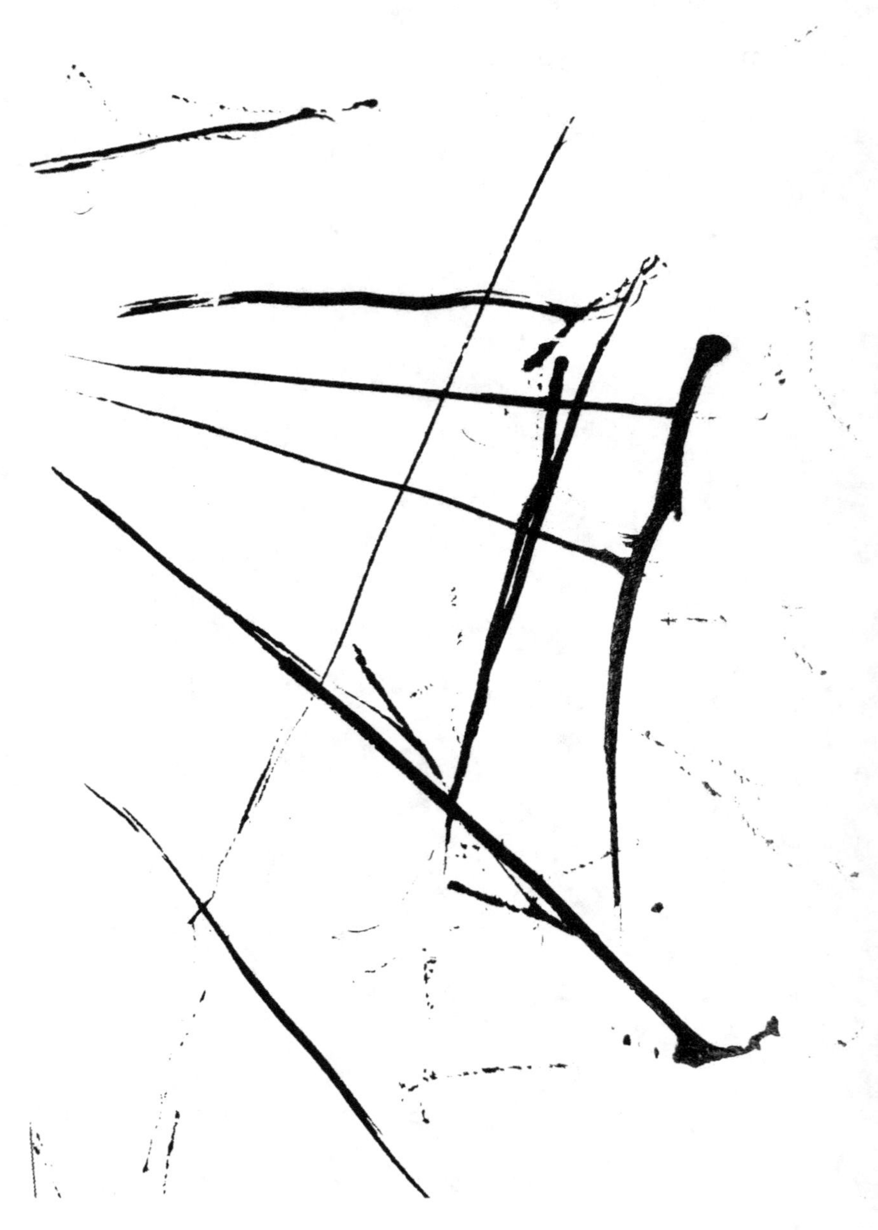

My name is ...

I am the messenger of ...

I am here to tell you ...

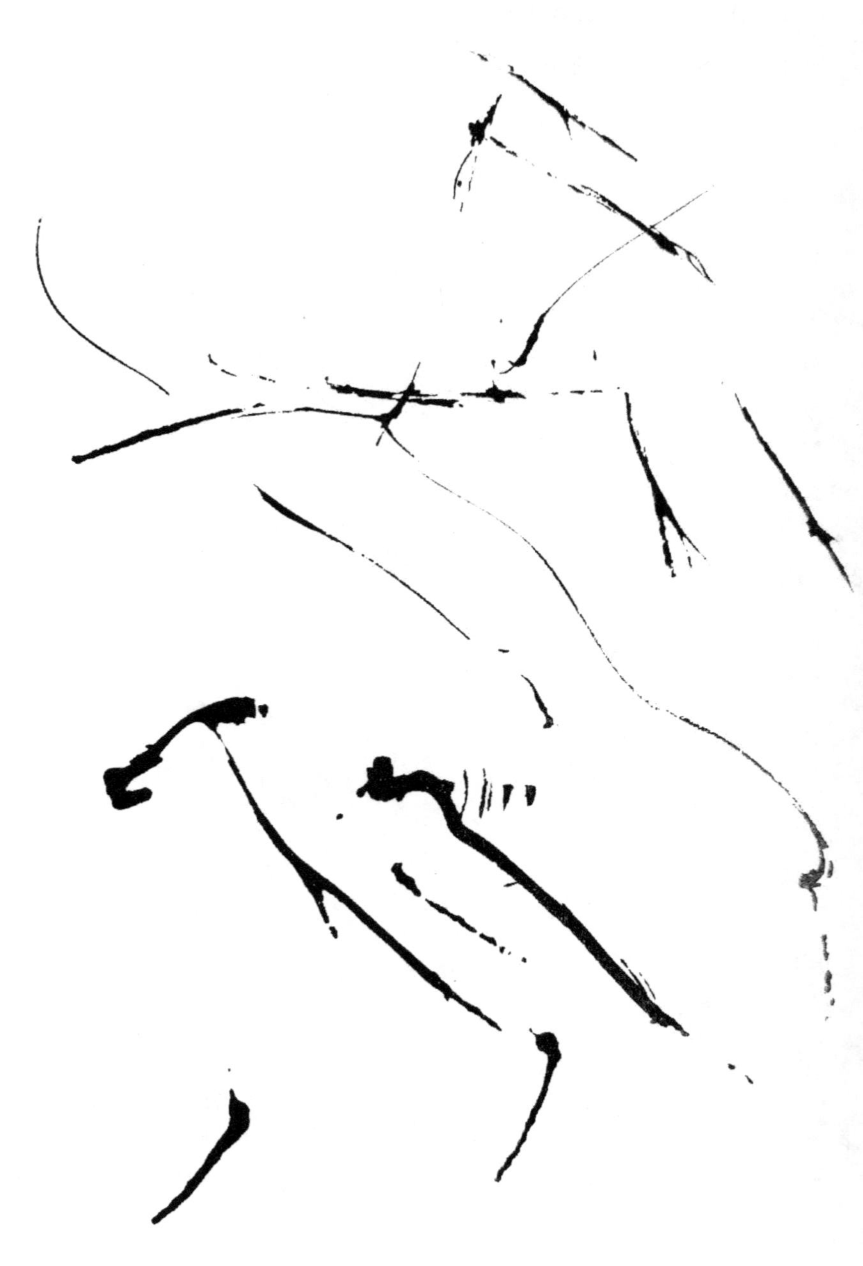

My name is ...

I am the messenger of ...

I am here to tell you ...

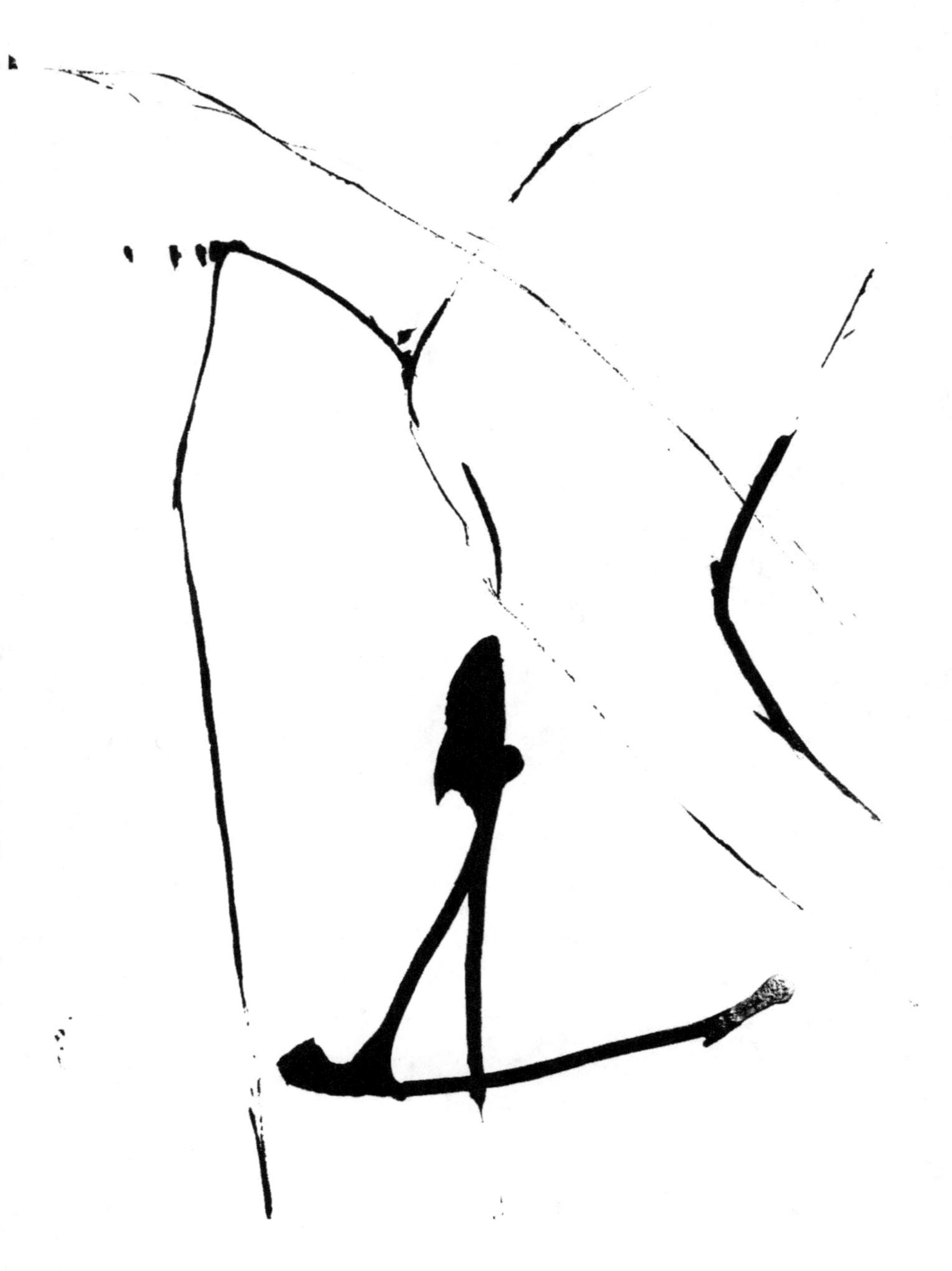

My name is ...

I am the messenger of ...

I am here to tell you ...

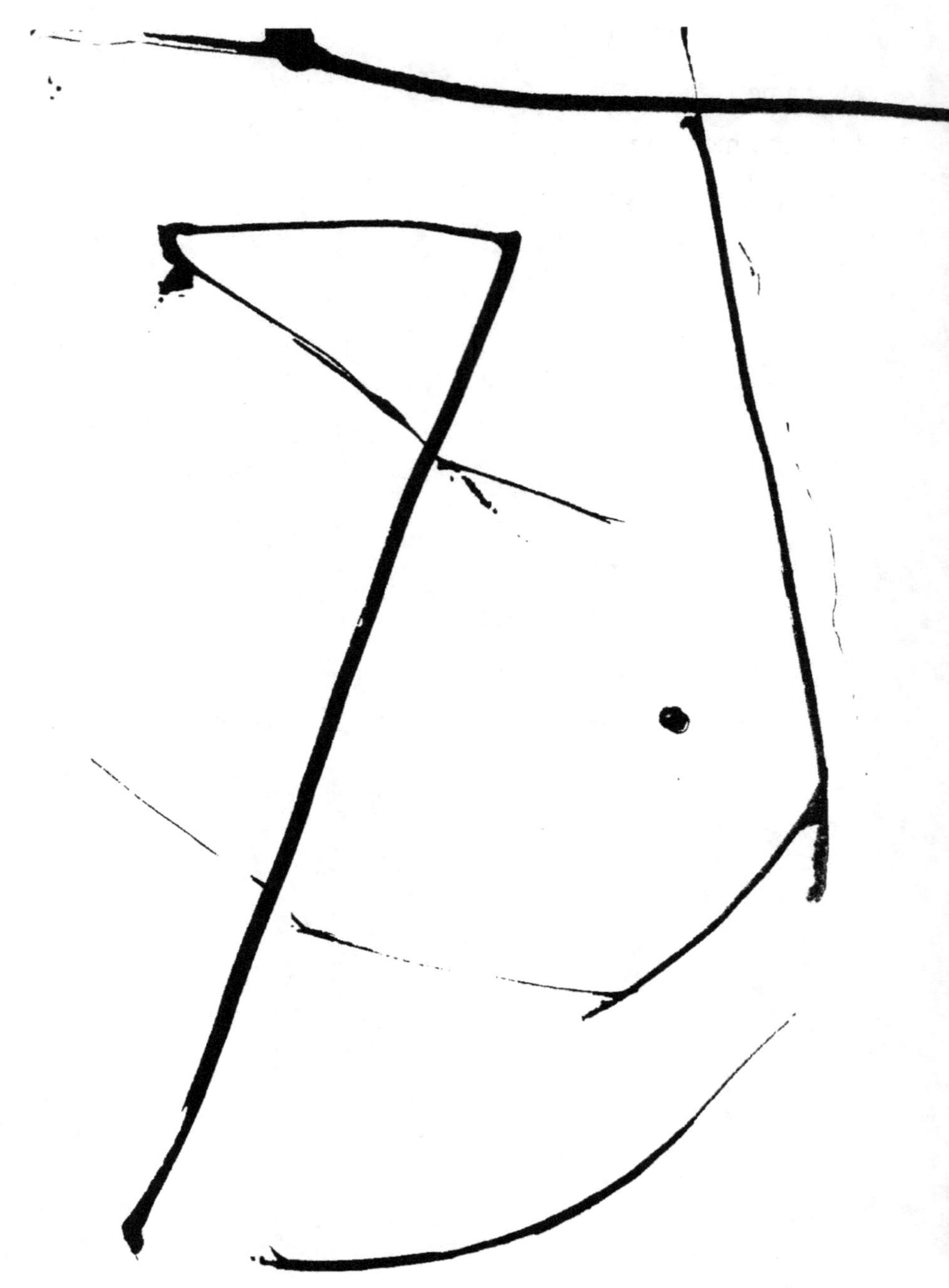

My name is ...

I am the messenger of ...

I am here to tell you ...

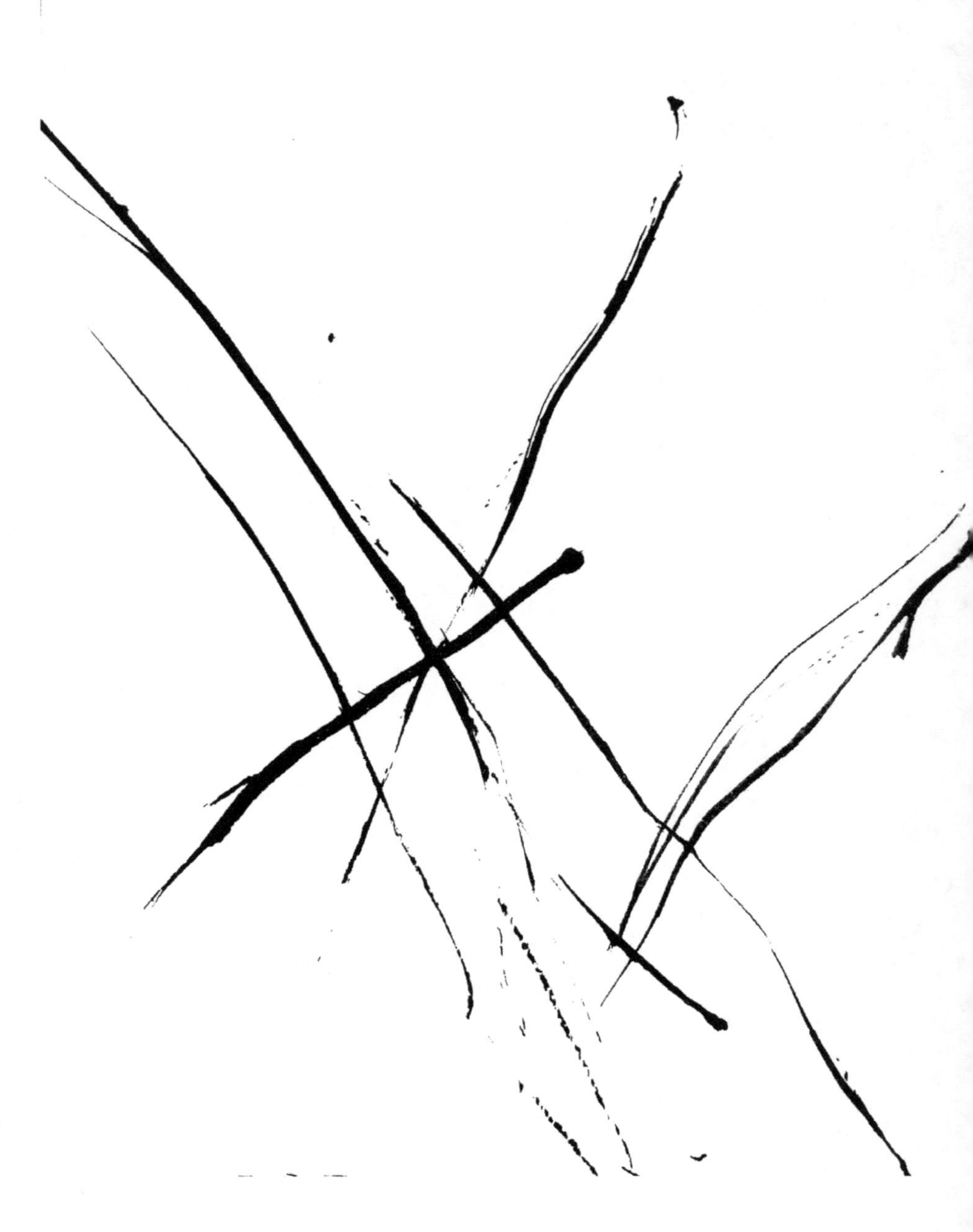

My name is ...

I am the messenger of ...

I am here to tell you ...

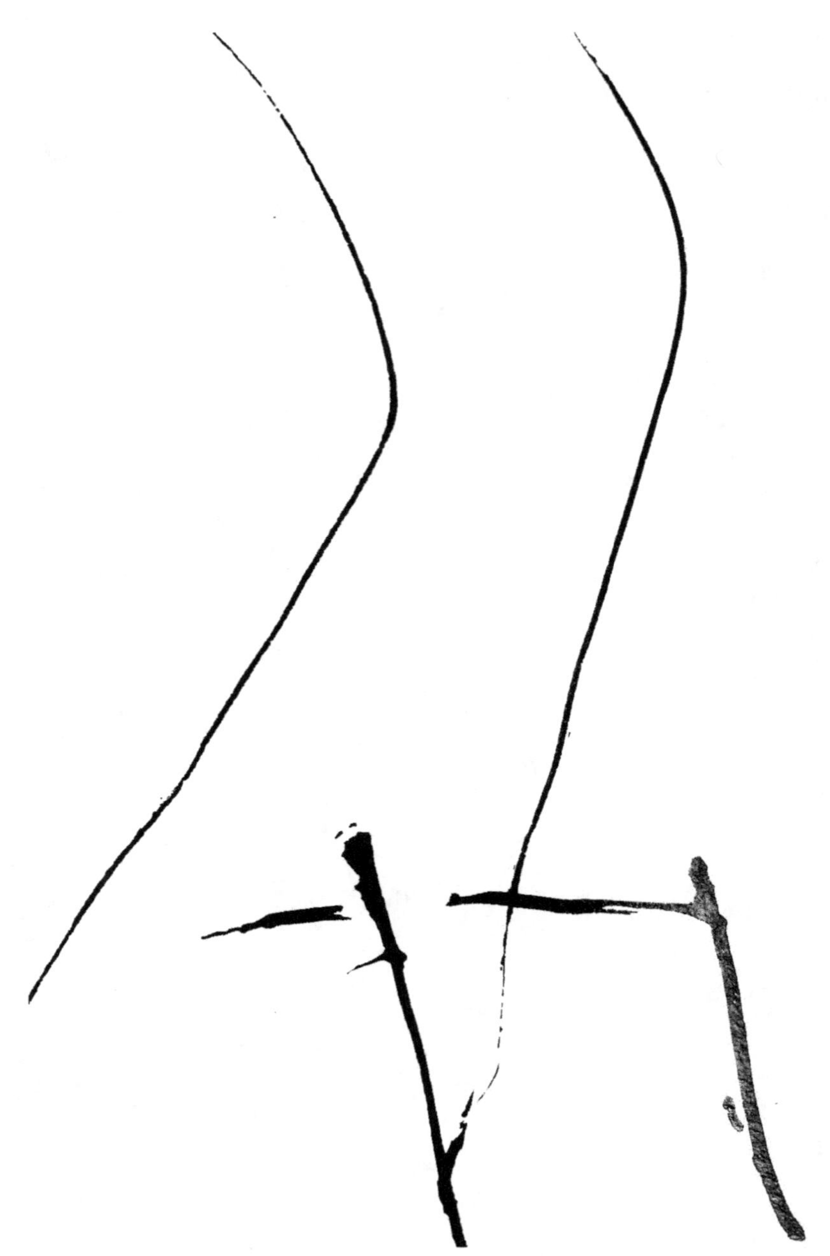

My name is ...

I am the messenger of ...

I am here to tell you ...

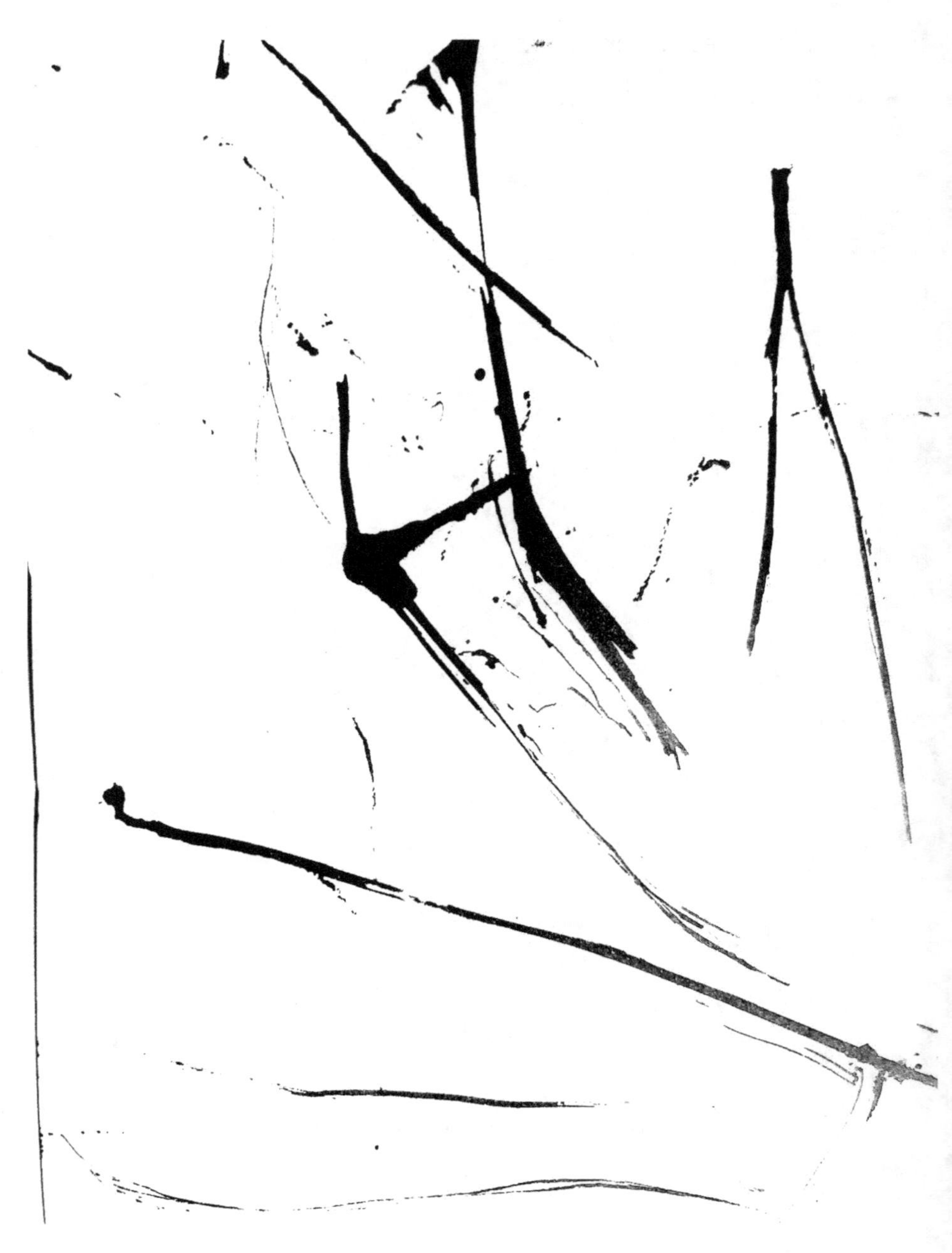

My name is ...

I am the messenger of ...

I am here to tell you ...

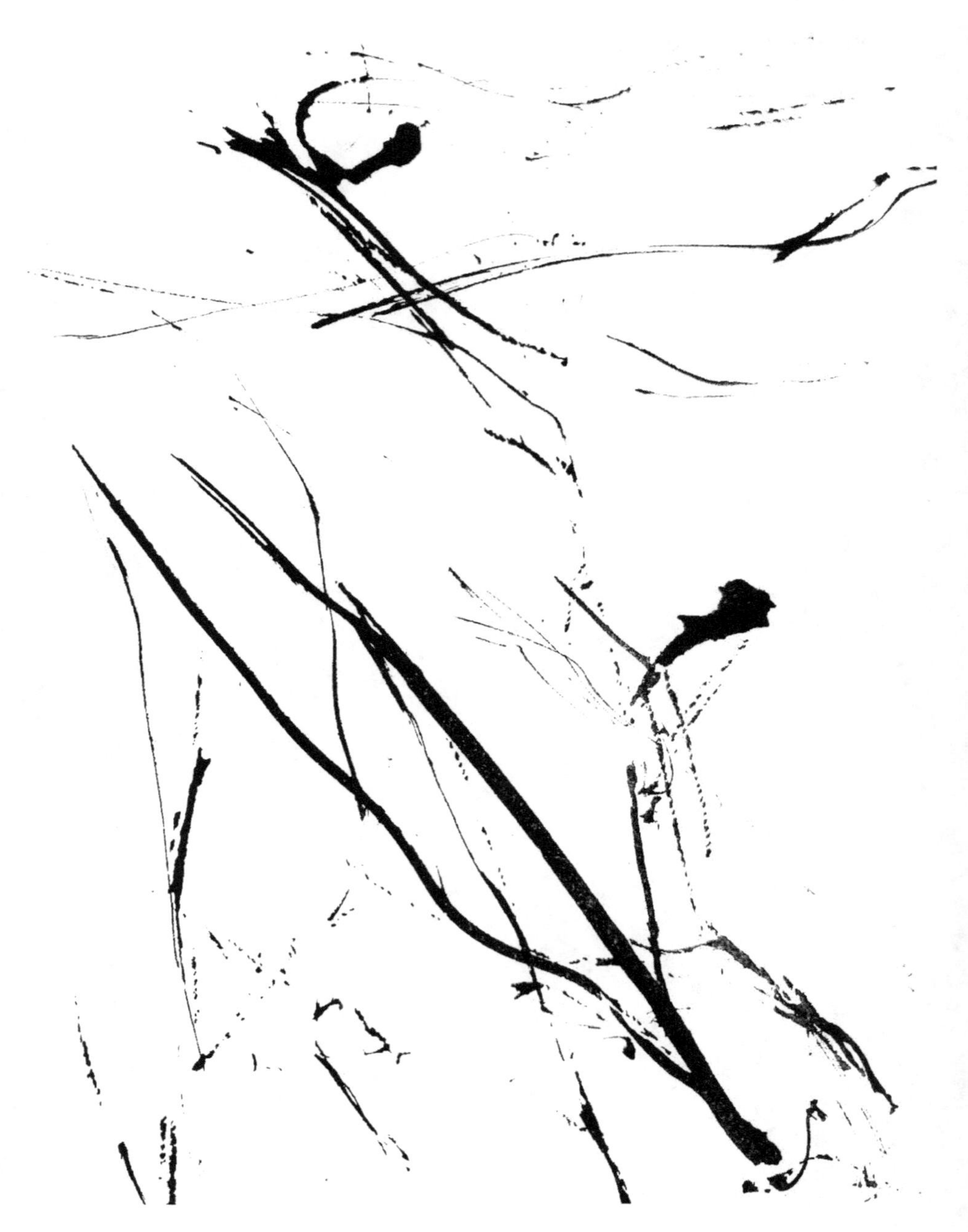

My name is ...

I am the messenger of ...

I am here to tell you ...

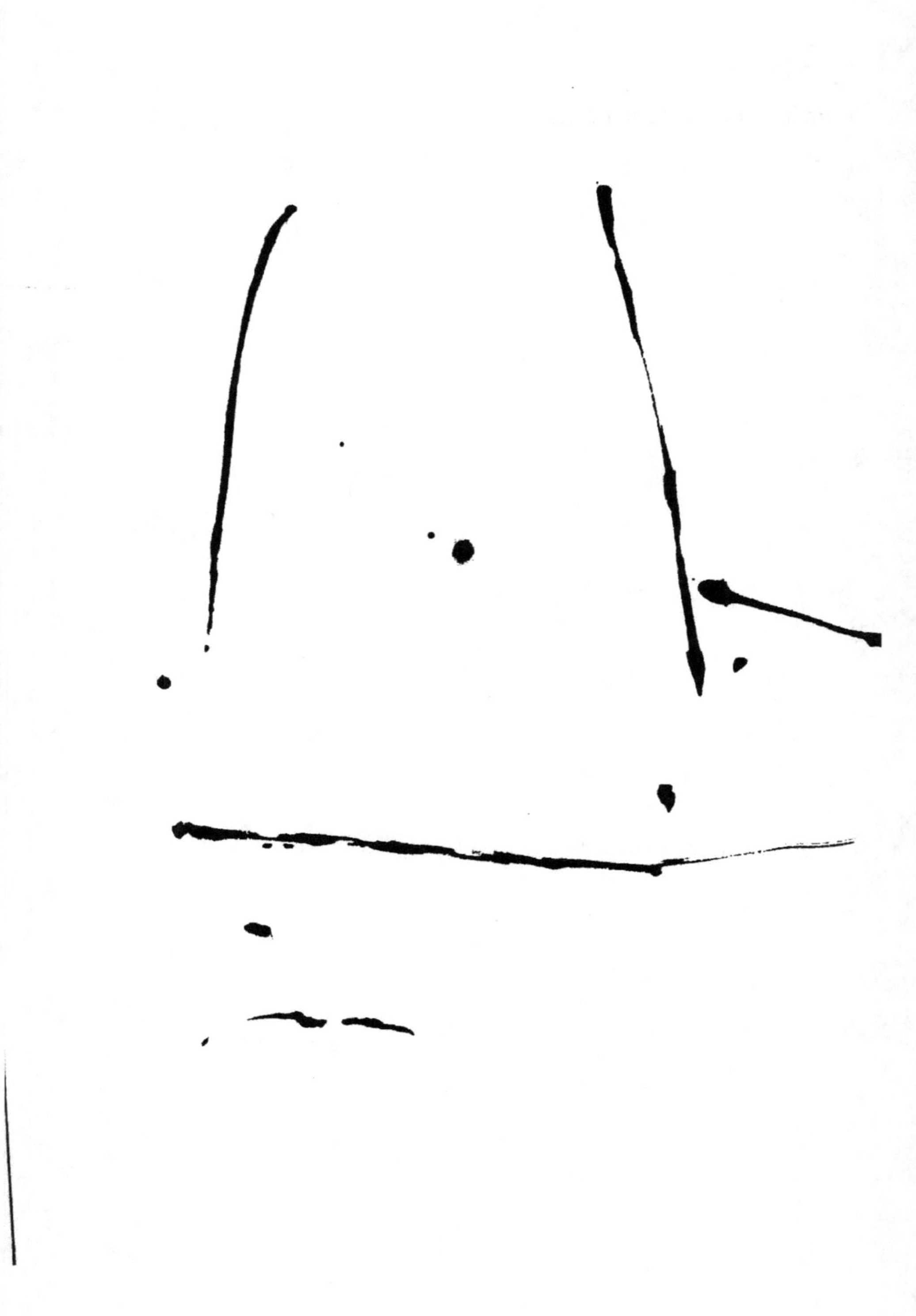

My name is ...

I am the messenger of ...

I am here to tell you ...

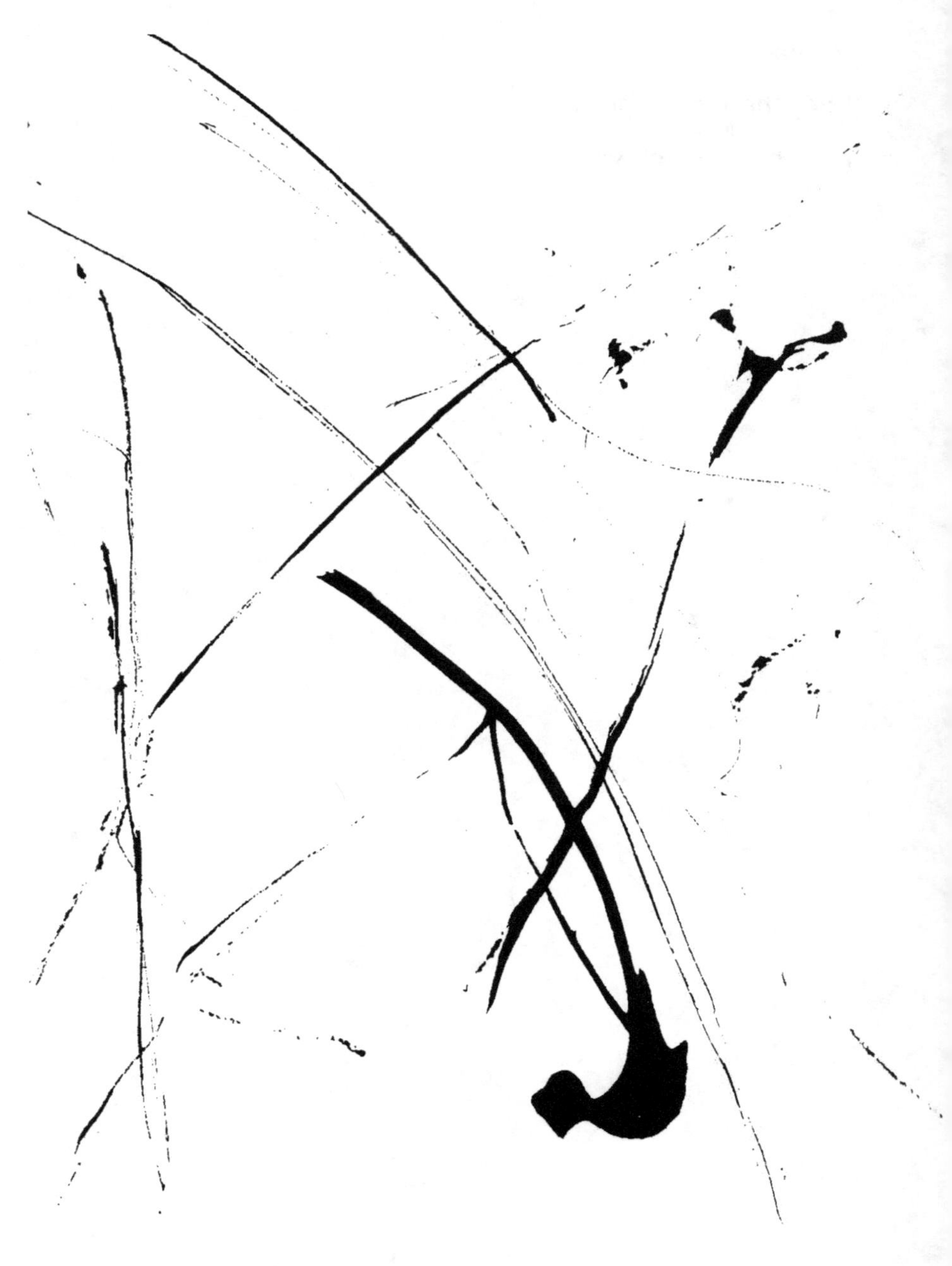

My name is ...

I am the messenger of ...

I am here to tell you ...

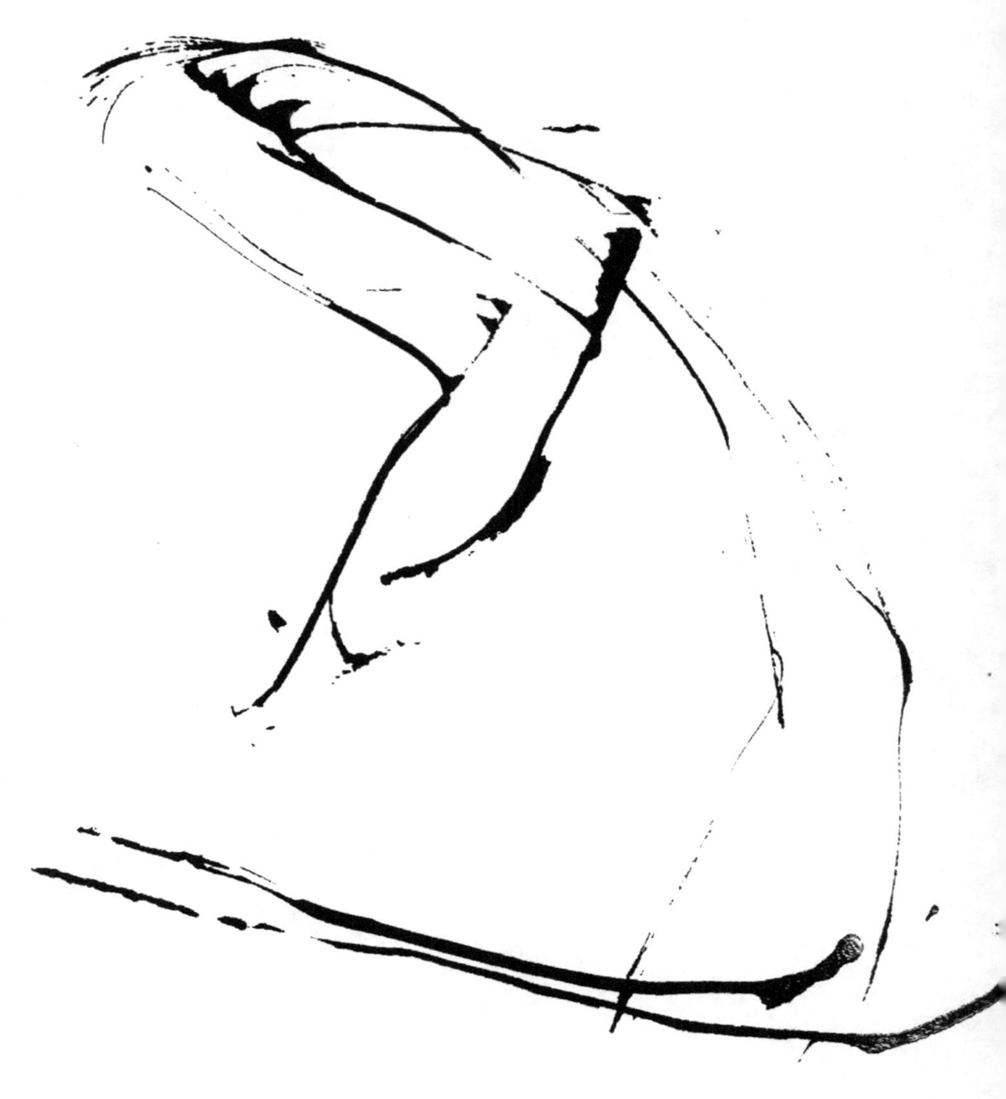

My name is ...

I am the messenger of ...

I am here to tell you ...

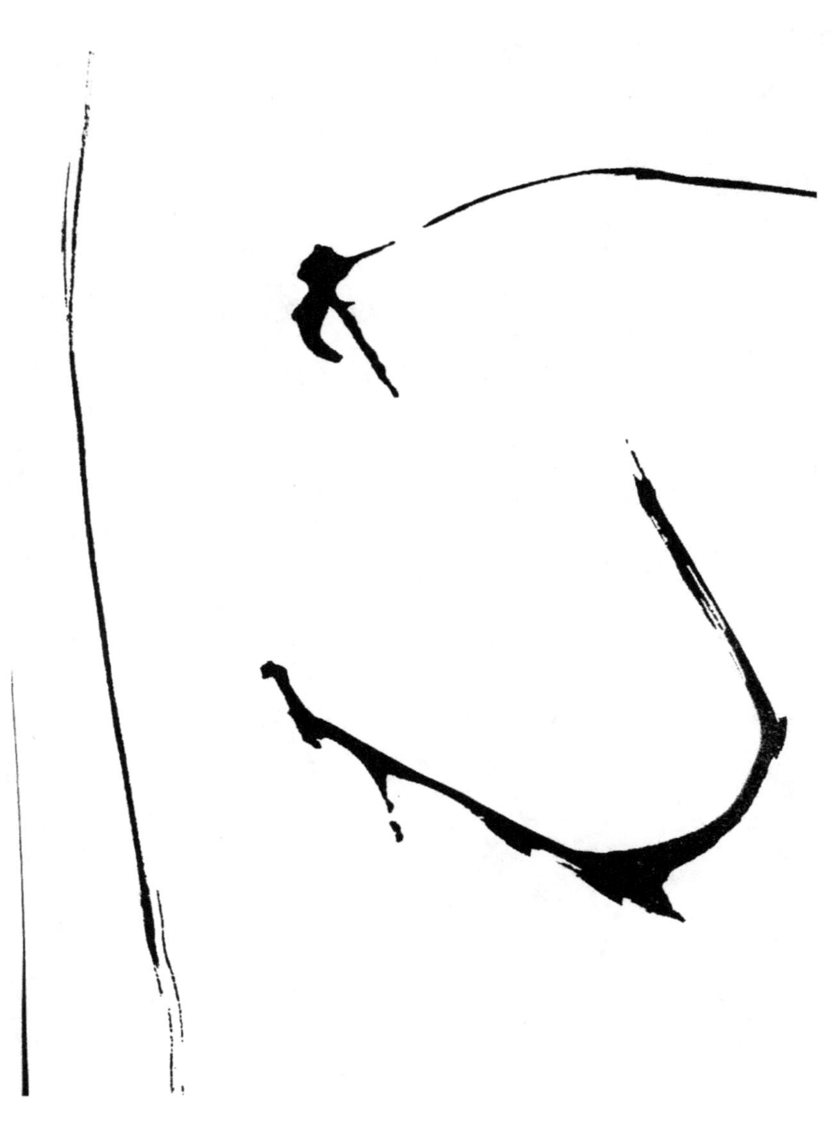

My name is ...

I am the messenger of ...

I am here to tell you ...

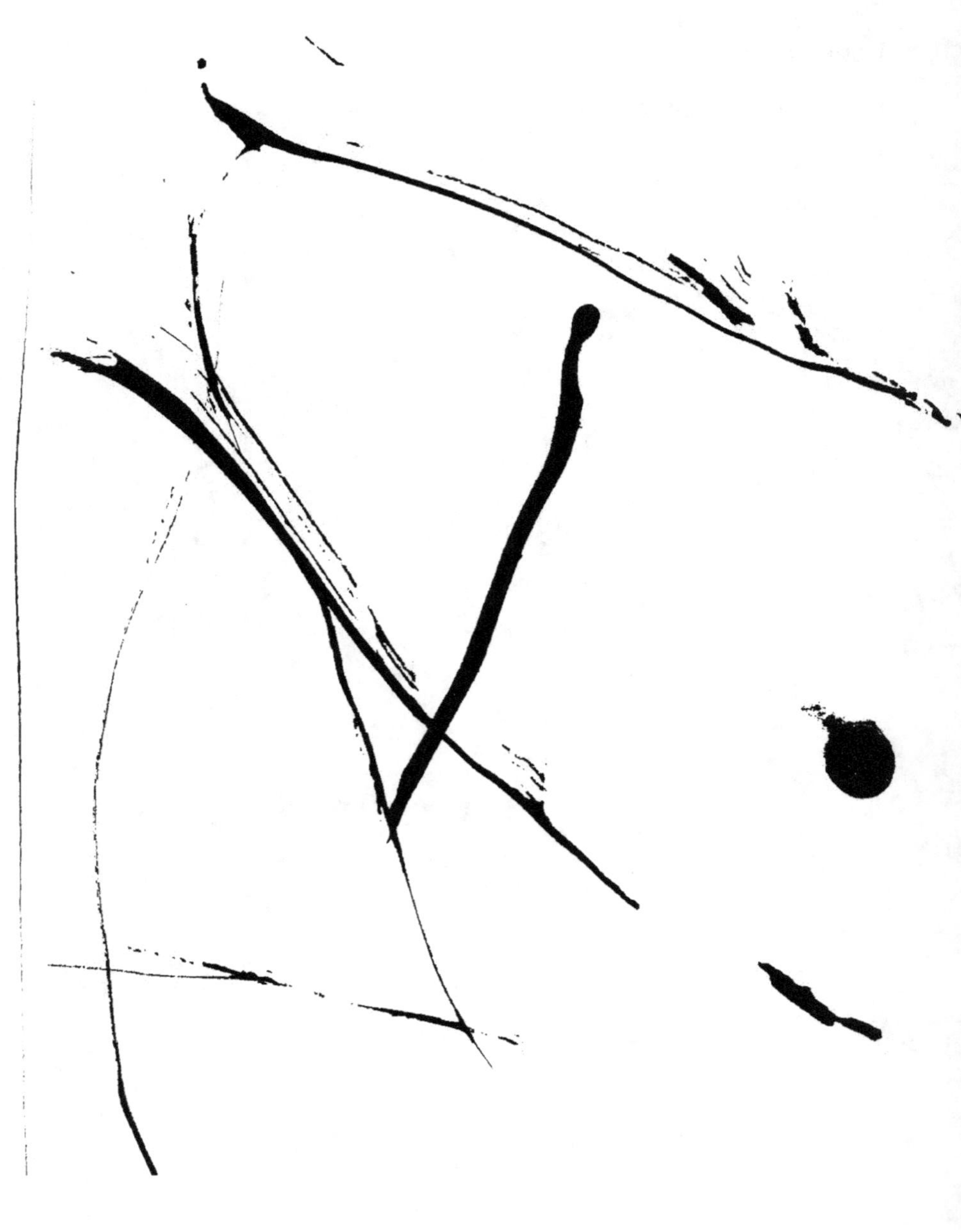

My name is ...

I am the messenger of ...

I am here to tell you ...

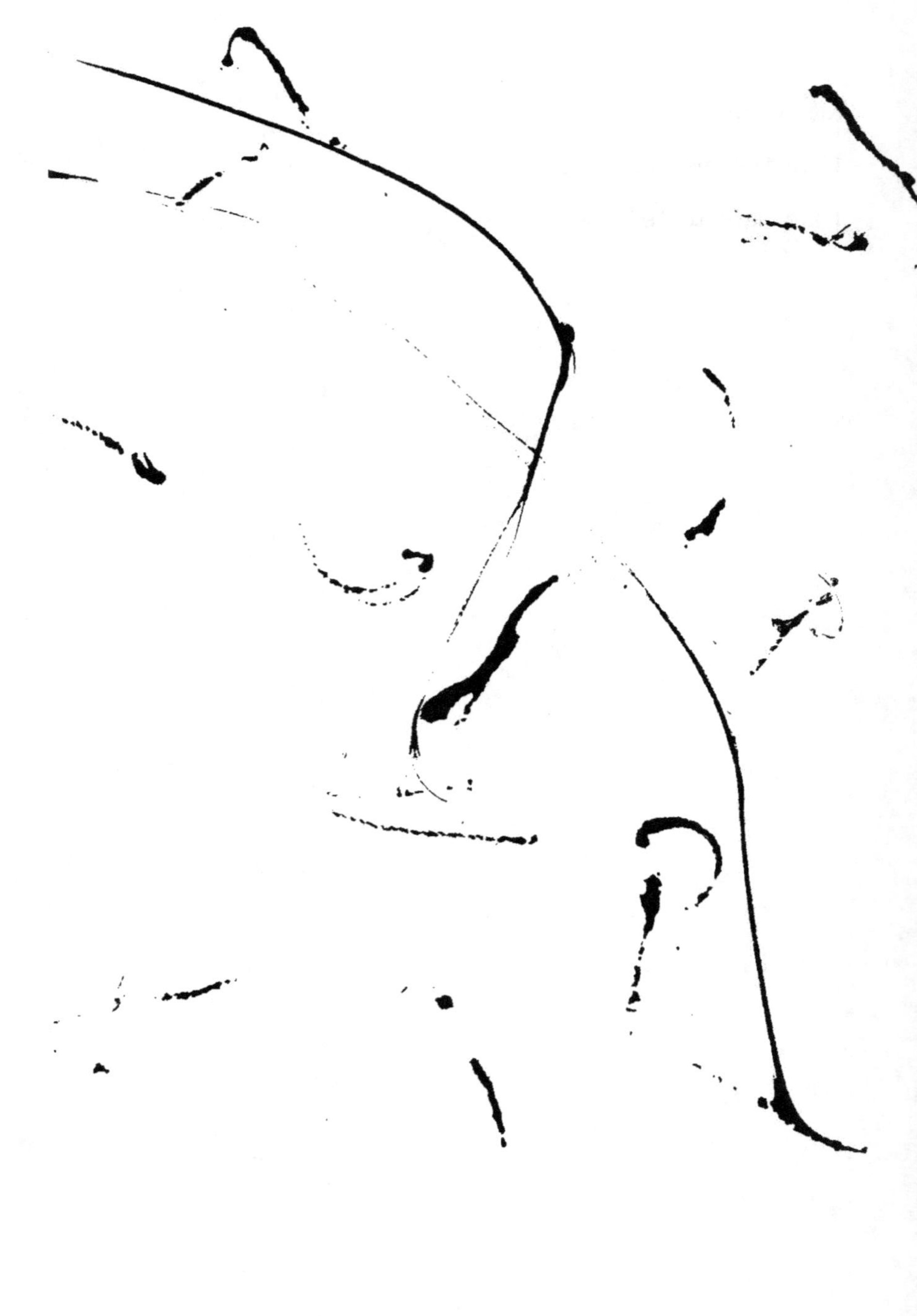

My name is ...

I am the messenger of ...

I am here to tell you ...

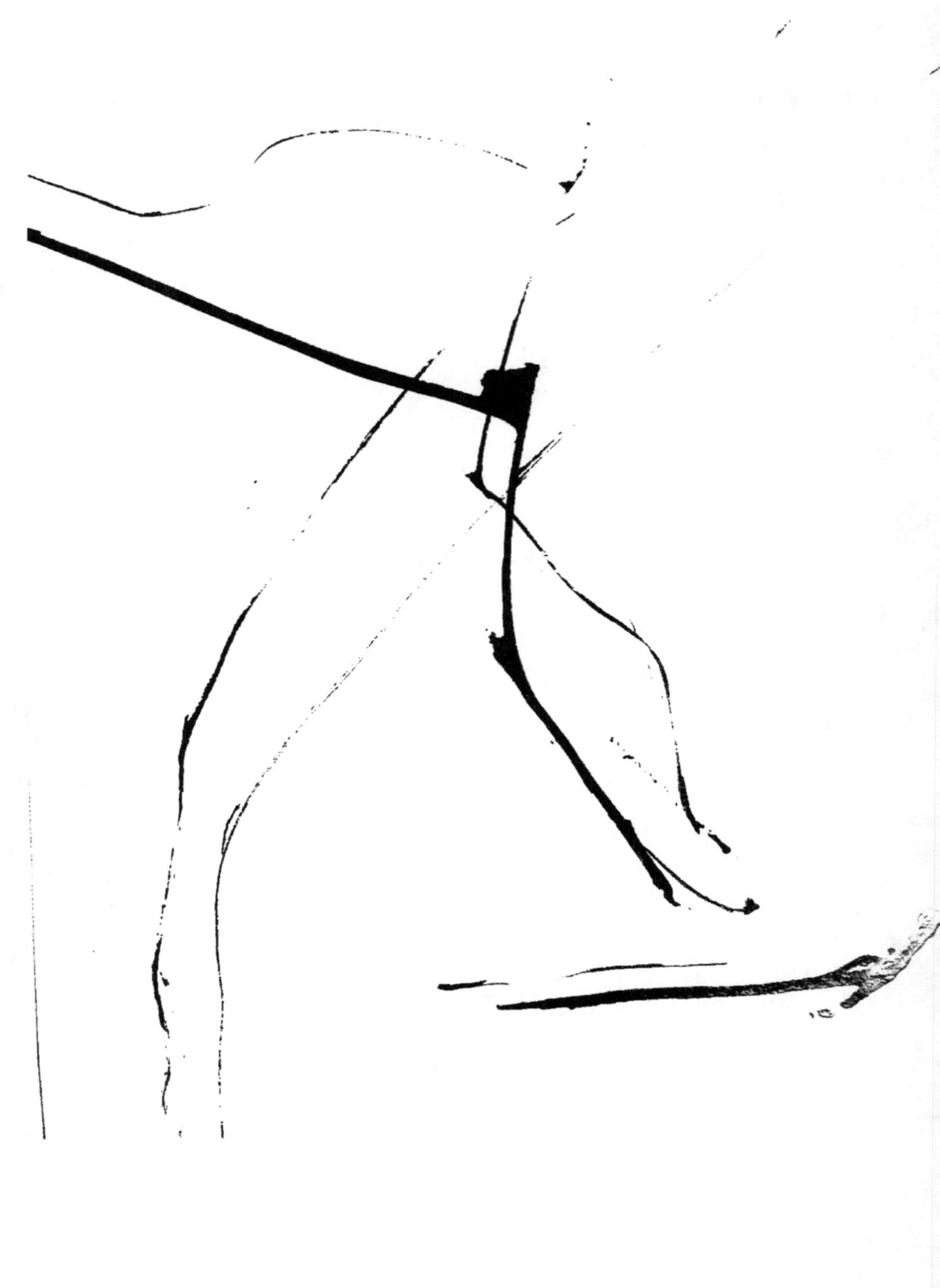

My name is ...

I am the messenger of ...

I am here to tell you ...

www.ingramcontent.com/pod-product-compliance
Lightning Source LLC
LaVergne TN
LVHW020312110826
845148LV00017BA/2644

9781734785036